MW01488691

A Mom's Book of Blessing

THIS BOOK BELONGS TO

Find us on Facebook and join the community of moms!
facebook.com/WhereMomsConnect

Loveland, Colorado | group.com

Group resources really work!

This Group resource incorporates our R.E.A.L. approach to ministry. It reinforces a growing friendship with Jesus, encourages long-term learning, and results in life transformation, because it's:

Relational—Learner-to-learner interaction enhances learning and builds Christian friendships.

Experiential—What learners experience through discussion and action sticks with them up to 9 times longer than what they simply hear or read.

Applicable—The aim of Christian education is to equip learners to be both hearers and doers of God's Word.

Learner-based—Learners understand and retain more when the learning process takes into consideration how they learn best.

A Mom's Book of Blessing

Copyright © 2015 Group Publishing, Inc.

All rights reserved. No part of this book may be reproduced in any manner whatsoever without prior written permission from the publisher, except where noted in the text and in the case of brief quotations embodied in critical articles and reviews. For information, go to group.com/permissions.

Visit our website: **group.com/women**

This resource is brought to you by the wildly creative women's ministry team at Group. Additional moms who contributed to this book include:

Jean Blackmer
Tamara Collins
Linda Crawford
Natalie Gillespie
Jill Wuellner

Unless otherwise indicated, all Scripture quotations are taken from the *Holy Bible*, New Living Translation, copyright © 1996, 2004, 2007, 2013 by Tyndale House Foundation. Used by permission of Tyndale House Publishers, Inc., Carol Stream, Illinois 60188. All rights reserved.

ISBN 978-1-4707-2406-1

Printed in the United States of America.

10 9 8 7 6 5 4 3 2 1   24 23 22 21 20 19 18 17 16 15

···· Contents ····

Welcome to ....A Year of....
BLESSING

As a mom, some days it's easy to count blessings—
snuggles with your little one during morning cartoons
or a surprise call home from your college freshman.
But on other days, like when the flu hits or homework gets
forgotten, it's a bit more challenging.

This year as you join with other moms at Where Moms
Connect, you'll explore how to find thanks for the good days
and the not-so-good days and how to be a blessing to others.
And through it all, you'll also find encouragement to lift your
heart and encouragement in your relationship with God.

This book will be your guide every step of the way. Tucked
in these pages are all the notes, Bible verses, reflections, and
other content you'll need to participate each time you gather
at Where Moms Connect. Be sure to bring this book along
when you meet.

We know that as a mom you're busy. But we also know
you care about growing yourself spiritually, emotionally,
and mentally. So along with the content for each session of
Where Moms Connect, we've included additional notes for
you to read and reflect on if you have time. Sometimes it's
a devotion, sometimes a few verses, other times just a short
thought to reflect on. These are for you to use as you want,
as you have time, with no guilt and no pressure.

Thanks for joining other moms at Where Moms Connect.
We hope this truly is a year of blessing for you on your
journey in momhood!

A Life of Blessing

Connecting to the Topic

Counting Blessings

Discuss:

• What's the strangest, funniest, or maybe yuckiest heartfelt gift you've received from a child? Tell your group!

_____

_____

_____

• What made such odd and sometimes yucky gifts a blessing instead of an unwanted gift?

because it's given with uninhibited

love.

_____

What's a Blessing?

A common dictionary definition of the word _blessing_ is:

A beneficial thing for which one is grateful; something that brings well-being.

Discuss:

- What can make you feel like your blessing jar has been dumped out?

  progress to only revert back

- When have you experienced something that you weren't happy or thankful for at first, but it later became a blessing in your life? Share a "blessing-in-disguise" story with your group.

Other dictionary definitions for the word *blessing* include:

God's favor and protection.

A prayer asking for God's favor or protection.

A person's sanction or support.

Discuss:

- How do these added definitions help you in recognizing blessings in your life?

  It's in the details!

Connecting With God

God gave a promise to bless us when he promised Abraham:

"All the families on earth will be blessed through you."
(Genesis 12:3)

"So all who put their faith in Christ share the same blessing Abraham received because of his faith." (Galatians 3:9)

Have one mom in your group read the following verses aloud, and then discuss the questions that are below.

"Then Jesus turned to his disciples and said, 'God blesses you who are poor, for the Kingdom of God is yours. God blesses you who are hungry now, for you will be satisfied. God blesses you who weep now, for in due time you will laugh.

"What blessings await you when people hate you and exclude you and mock you and curse you as evil because you follow the Son of Man.'" (Luke 6:20-22)

- How do you think God can turn the difficult things listed in this Bible passage into blessings in our lives?

This too shall pass...

In the Old Testament part of the Bible, the terms for blessing are related to the word meaning "to kneel." Because the knees were considered a weak part of the body, a person would become "weak" before God by kneeling to receive a blessing.

"God blesses those who are poor and realize their need for him, for the Kingdom of Heaven is theirs." (Matthew 5:3)

- How can becoming "weak" before God help us to receive blessings in our lives?

humility goes a long way!

Connecting to My Life

"All praise to God, the Father of our Lord Jesus Christ, who has blessed us with every spiritual blessing in the heavenly realms because we are united with Christ." (Ephesians 1:3)

Use this space to journal your thoughts, draw a picture, write words of thankfulness, or capture any inspirations you want to remember from today.

Mercy
Grace
BLESSINGS

"Bless—that's your job, to bless. You'll be a blessing and also get a blessing." (1 Peter 3:9, The Message)

Additional Thoughts on a Life of Blessing

"All must give as they are able, according to the blessings given to them by the Lord your God." (Deuteronomy 16:17)

When I attended the University of North Carolina at Chapel Hill there was a beautiful common area on campus surrounded by trees and flowering plants. During the spring, in particular, I would make a point to walk through the area on my way to Franklin Street's coffee shops and other college hangouts. In the shade of massive oaks, the aroma of honeysuckle and lilac was intoxicating, and the experience was both old and new each time I made my way across the beautiful expanse.

On a particularly warm spring day as I crossed the common on my way to meet my study group, I heard what sounded like someone playing a saxophone off in the distance. I followed the sound for about five minutes until I saw the source of the sound.

It was indeed someone playing a sax. And I do mean playing. About 30 feet away on a corner of the street stood a round little man in khaki shorts, a Hawaiian shirt, and a pith helmet. And he was making that tenor sax sing. He was obviously a jazz player from way back.

I walked closer, mesmerized. The notes cascaded around the gathering crowd in an effortless stream, and you could feel the raw emotion in the strains of "Amazing Grace." From there he launched into an equally powerful arrangement of "A Quiet Place," and no one moved.

We just stood there, transfixed.

After a few minutes, he opened the case at his feet, took out a red bandana, and wiped his face. As he took off the pith helmet and wiped his bald head, I took out a dollar and dropped it in his case. As I walked away, he called out, "Hey, man, don't do that."

He picked up the dollar and held it out to me. "Here, cat." (Now I *knew* he was a jazz man.) "Put this back in your pocket," he said.

"No," I replied. "That's for you. You were really making that sax wail. In fact, I could stand here and listen to you play all afternoon."

He tucked the dollar in my shirt pocket and grinned, "Then that's payment enough."

I looked at him for a long moment and shook my head. "I don't get it," I said. "There are always musicians out here playing for money. And you're the best I've heard."

"I appreciate that, and you're very kind to say so," he said, "but I'm not playing for the money."

"Then why are you playing?"

He smiled and tightened the ligature screws. "Because I can." He adjusted the mouthpiece and said, "You see, God gave me a gift, and this is my way of giving a little something back to him."

T. Smith

• How can you bless someone today—just because you can, with no hope of anything in return?

I gave a free haircut to a Vet not expecting anything in return. Just to say "Thank you for your service & sacrifice." He tipped me anyway.

How to Be Grateful—
And Raise Grateful Children

Connecting Together

Discuss:

• What's one thing you're thankful for today?

<u>My family. I would be bored otherwise!</u>
<u>They are my everything in this</u>
<u>world. They help me look up to the</u>
<u>Heavens!</u>

• When it comes to how thankful you've felt lately, would you say you're a glass that's full, a glass that's half empty, or a glass that's bone dry?

<u>Half full - there's</u>
<u>always room for</u>
<u>more.</u>

• How thankful have you felt lately—and why?

_____

_____

_____

Connecting to the Topic

Seasons

Discuss:

• Tell about a time in your life when it was hard for you to feel thankful.

_____

_____

_____

_____

Thankfulness helps us refocus on what we have rather than on what we lack, and studies indicate that thankfulness brings some very real benefits:

• More likely to meet goals

• More alert and enthusiastic

• More helpful

• Healthier

• Happier

   "Gratitude lifts me up in the times I've struggled and grounds me when things are going well." —Trista Sutter

• What impact has gratitude had in your life? Or haven't you noticed that it has?

_____

_____

_____

_____

Thankfulness Ideas to Try:

Which of these ideas might you want to try? Put a star next to any of the suggestions that you might do this week.

Why We're Thankful For...

Discuss:

- Who's someone not in the room you're thankful for? Why are you thankful for that person?

_____

_____

_____

Connecting With God

Surveys show that about 90 percent of Americans pray daily or almost every day.

Discuss:

- How many of your conversations with God are about asking for something, and how many are about being thankful?

_____

_____

_____

_____

- How might expressing more thankfulness affect your relationship with God?

_____

_____

_____

_____

"Be cheerful no matter what; pray all the time; thank God no matter what happens. This is the way God wants you who belong to Christ Jesus to live."
(1 Thessalonians 5:16-18, _The Message_)

Connecting to My Life

Dear God, I'm thankful for…

Additional Thoughts on How to Be Grateful

"Be thankful in all circumstances, for this is God's will for you who belong to Christ Jesus." (1 Thessalonians 5:18)

I asked a preschooler, "What are you thankful for?"

He replied, "I don't know what thankful is, but I know 'thank full' is better than 'thank empty.'"

Everyone is thankful about something, and everyone is ungrateful about something. It's up to us to draw the lines where we want to be. Anything we look at can be seen through a lens of gratefulness or ungratefulness. You can choose to be more full or more empty.

The line in the grocery store can be seen as a frustrating waste of time, or it can be seen as an opportunity to spend time in thought and to be grateful for shelves so full of food.

The lack of sleep from a crying baby can be seen as wear and tear on a day and a reason to breed crabbiness, or it can be seen as a night that no one else in the entire world will ever get to experience. It can be a night where a young child is loved in a way that no one else would ever love them. It is a night where the safety of a warm house, ample water and food, and the dawn of a new day can bring overwhelming gratitude.

The guy who cuts you off in traffic could be described with adjectives that fingers should not type on a keyboard. He can be a cause for raised blood pressure and revenge. But this same guy can be seen as a way to get your attention and be grateful you have the physical ability to maneuver a car. Many do not. Only a small percentage of the world's population even owns a car, and you are one of that small, privileged percentage.

When God asks us to be thankful in all circumstances, he wants us to be truly full and never fully empty.

Fill a glass of water only half full. Imagine yourself very thirsty, and thank God for the water. Are you thanking him for what is there? Or focusing on what's missing? What can you do to concentrate on the fullness of thanks and not the emptiness?

Sheila Halasz

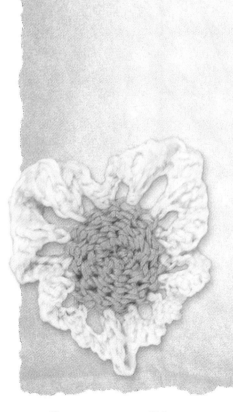

Helping Your Children Discover Their
Gifts and *Talents*

Connecting to the Topic

Discuss:

• What are a few qualities and character traits you would like to see your children develop?

_____

_____

_____

_____

• What have you done in your home to help your kids develop one or more of those qualities?

_____

_____

_____

_____

Connecting With God

One mom can read this verse aloud:

"But the Holy Spirit produces this kind of fruit in our lives: love, joy, peace, patience, kindness, goodness, faithfulness, gentleness, and self-control. There is no law against these things! Those who belong to Christ Jesus have nailed the passions and desires of their sinful nature to his cross and crucified them there. Since we are living by the Spirit, let us follow the Spirit's leading in every part of our lives. Let us not become conceited, or provoke one another, or be jealous of one another." (Galatians 5:22-26)

Discuss:

• How are the fruits of the Spirit different than the character traits often taught in our culture such as respect, responsibility, trustworthiness, fairness, or others that you listed earlier?

_____

_____

_____

• Why is it significant to know these are given by God and not something we acquire and perfect?

_____

_____

_____

• Why do you think it's important we teach our kids these are qualities that God says matter?

_____

_____

_____

Have one mom read this Bible passage aloud:

"For you created my inmost being; you knit me together in my mother's womb. I praise you because I am fearfully and wonderfully made; your works are wonderful, I know that full well. My frame was not hidden from you when I was made in the secret place. When I was woven together in the depths of the earth, your eyes saw my unformed body. All the days ordained for me were written in your book before one of them came to be." (Psalm 139:13-16, NIV)

Discuss:

- How might it change your child's perspective if they understood that God made them perfectly with the exact talents and abilities he wanted them to have? How might it change your perspective as a mom?

_____

_____

_____

Connecting to My Life

- Love

_____

_____

- Joy

_____

_____

- Peace

_____

_____

- Patience

_____

_____

- Kindness

_____

_____

- Goodness

_____

_____

- Faithfulness

_____

_____

- Gentleness

_____

_____

- Self-Control

_____

_____

Additional Thoughts on Helping Your Children Discover Their Gifts and Talents

Have you ever looked at someone and wished you could be like them? To have the patience of a certain friend or the ability to put together a wardrobe like the mom who always looks so fashionable? If we're honest, we all have looked at others and felt wishful, disappointed in ourselves, or dissatisfied with who we are. We put on the happy face, put our best foot forward, and hope others see something of value.

In his book *The Search for Significance*, Robert S. McGee writes, "Our true value is based not on our behavior or the approval of others but on what God's Word says is true of us" (pg. 19).

When we understand who God says we are, then we can fully display the fruits of the Spirit, as well as teach our kids the truth about who they are and the God who made them. So what does God say about you? Read the passages below and remind yourself of who you are in Christ. After each one, write a note to remind yourself of who God says you are.

• Colossians 2:13-14

_____

_____

• Romans 8:15

_____

_____

• 2 Corinthians 5:17

_____

_____

- 1 John 3:1

_____

_____

- Ephesians 2:10

_____

_____

- 2 Corinthians 5:21

_____

_____

- John 15:15

_____

_____

- Romans 5:1

_____

_____

- Colossians 3:12

_____

_____

- Romans 5:8

_____

_____

How to Be Happier

Connecting Together

Mingle, Mingle

When you hear the music, start to mingle! When the music stops, tell the mom you connected with something that made you happy today.

Discuss:

• How happy have you been feeling lately, and why?

_____

_____

_____

Connecting to the Topic

The Happiness Project

• A recent Harris Poll reports that only 1 in 3 Americans says he or she is very happy.

• Especially dissatisfied with their happiness levels are minorities, the disabled, and recent college graduates.

- Canadians ranked 6th in international happiness compared to Americans who placed 17th.

- Among people surveyed who'd suffered a financial setback, more than half said that their experience helped them realize what's truly important—and it's not money.

- One-third of our happiness level is determined by our genes, while two-thirds is determined by our attitude.

Connecting With God

"I know that there is nothing better for people than to be happy and to do good while they live. That each of them may eat and drink, and find satisfaction in all their toil—this is the gift of God." (Ecclesiastes 3:12-13, NIV)

Connecting to My Life

12 Happiness Tips From God

1. "You have shown me the paths of life; your presence will fill me with happiness." (Acts 2:28, CEB)

2. "I know that there is nothing better for people than to be happy and to do good while they live. That each of them may eat and drink, and find satisfaction in all their toil—this is the gift of God." (Ecclesiastes 3:12-13, NIV)

3. "Happy are people who are hopeless, because the kingdom of heaven is theirs." (Matthew 5:3, CEB)

4. "Happy are people who grieve, because they will be made glad." (Matthew 5:4, CEB)

5. "Happy are people who are humble, because they will inherit the earth." (Matthew 5:5, CEB)

6. "Happy are people who are hungry and thirsty for righteousness, because they will be fed until they are full." (Matthew 5:6, CEB)

7. "Happy are people who show mercy, because they will receive mercy." (Matthew 5:7, CEB)

8. "Happy are people who have pure hearts, because they will see God." (Matthew 5:8, CEB)

9. "Happy are people who make peace, because they will be called God's children." (Matthew 5:9, CEB)

10. "Happy are people whose lives are harassed because they are righteous, because the kingdom of heaven is theirs." (Matthew 5:10, CEB)

11. "Make me walk along the path of your commands, for that is where my happiness is found." (Psalm 119:35)

12. "It is the same with you. Now you are sad, but I will see you again and you will be happy, and no one will take away your joy." —Jesus (John 16:22, NCV)

12 Happiness Tips From Gretchen

1. Think "happier," not "happiness." Happiness isn't a finish line. It's a process, not a magical destination.

2. Build strong relationships. Deepen and broaden relationships. They give you a place to belong and confide.

3. Get—and give—support. Both give you happiness— especially helping others.

4. Be around people. Introvert or extrovert, you'll get a lift from social interaction. Engage with others.

5. Focus on your home. Take steps toward greater happiness there first.

6. Declutter. Cleaning up your living space and schedule opens up space for happiness.

7. Initiate a "threshold ritual." Upon entering or leaving your home, pause to be thankful.

8. Abandon a project. Never going to learn origami or finish that novel? Let yourself off the hook.

9. Cultivate good smells. What scents give you pleasure? Surround yourself with them.

10. Give warm greetings and farewells. Hugs, handshakes, kisses—give proper hellos and goodbyes.

11. Embrace gratitude. Gratitude drives out negative feelings.

12. Be specific—and accountable. Small steps toward happiness will carry you further if you're clear about what you'll do. Be specific; then measure your progress.

Tips I'd Like to Try...

Building Strong Relationships

With whom in your life do you want to be intentional about building a stronger relationship? Write that person's name here:

_____

Embrace Gratitude

Discuss:

• Tell about a time you were able to claim happiness after a time of hardship.

_____

_____

_____

_____

Additional Thoughts on How to Be Happier

1. **Get enough rest.** When you're exhausted, it's tough to be happy.

2. **Strap on the earphones.** Favorite music causes your brain to pump out dopamine, a neurotransmitter associated with happiness.

3. **De-screen.** A National Geographic survey found that people who watched less than one hour of television a day are happiest.

4. **Eat happy.** Add foods rich in tryptophan (which helps your body synthesize serotonin) to your diet. Try turkey, egg whites, black beans, walnuts, cashews, and almonds.

5. **Indulge in a little chocolate.** Just the smell of chocolate slows down brain waves and builds calm.

6. **Play.** An activity you enjoy—soccer, hiking, whatever—will build your happiness.

7. **Pay.** Generous behavior helps you feel better about yourself.

8. **Pray.** Ask God for help, and then relax—not worrying helps with happiness.

What ideas do you want to try? After you've done one or two of these, jot down your thoughts on how this helped (or didn't help) your happiness level.

_____

_____

_____

_____

_____

Service Projects for Families

Connecting Together

Discuss:

- On a scale of 1 to 10 (1 being little to none and 10 being fully able and ready to roll) what's your capacity to do a service project this week? Write your number and share with those at your table—and tell why you chose this number.

Connecting to the Topic

Ideas Galore!

- Make a no-sew fleece blanket to give to children in need of comfort. For instructions, search "how to make a no-sew fleece blanket" online.

- Make cards for people in the hospital or an elderly care facility.

- Write letters to a soldier. Operation Gratitude is a good website with instructions and the process for delivering letters to those serving overseas (operationgratitude.com/get-involved/how-you-can-help).

- Bake cookies or a casserole and take to a neighbor.

- Do yard work for an elderly neighbor or a neighbor with a disability. Or just do it for someone you want to surprise.

- Babysit for a mom who has a child with a disability. The whole family can enjoy playing with the child.

- Volunteer for Habitat for Humanity. (They do have age requirements so check with them before signing up young children.)

- Take a gift bag and fill it with items a child might enjoy for a birthday, and leave the bag at a shelter for families. Just because you're out of a home doesn't mean you don't have birthdays. ☺

- Make care packages for homeless people. Pack items such as granola bars, beef jerky, toothpaste and toothbrush, socks, gloves, and hats in a zip-seal bag. Keep these in your car, and they can be distributed whenever you see someone in need.

- Stock shelves at a local food bank.

- Host a fundraiser for a cause. Try a car wash, yard sale, or other idea, and donate all the profit to a cause your family cares about.

- Sponsor a child from Compassion International or another similar agency (compassion.com).

- Pack a shoebox for Operation Christmas Child (samaritanspurse.org).

- Get fit together. Join a race or bike ride as a family that benefits a cause you care about.

- Leave money on the vending machine for the next person.

- Leave an extra big tip for your wait person.

Now brainstorm some of your own ideas together. Write ideas you want to try here:

_____

_____

_____

_____

_____

Motivate Me!

"Let us think of ways to motivate one another to acts of love and good works." (Hebrews 10:24)

Ideas on how to motivate my family to serve:

_____

_____

_____

_____

_____

Connecting With God

Ask one woman to read this verse aloud to the table group; then discuss the questions below.

"For we are God's masterpiece. He has created us anew in Christ Jesus, so we can do the good things he planned for us long ago." (Ephesians 2:10)

• What does it mean to you that you are God's "masterpiece"?

_____

_____

_____

• How does this verse cause you to think about God equipping you to do good works?

_____

_____

_____

"You should remember the words of the Lord Jesus: 'It is more blessed to give than to receive.'" (Acts 20:35)

- When have you experienced the blessing of giving—and felt it was better than actually receiving?

_____

_____

_____

Connecting to My Life

"Find a need and fill it."

Ruth Stafford Peale, who was the wife of Reverend Norman Vincent Peale (author of *The Power of Positive Thinking*), is credited with this quote. It was a motto she lived by until her death at the age of 101 in 2008.

As you reflect on this quote, and the conversations we've had today, what do you feel are your next steps? Journal about what acts of love and good deeds you feel motivated to do with your family, or write other insights you've had from our time today.

_____

_____

_____

_____

_____

_____

_____

_____

Additional Thoughts on Service Projects for Families

"And let us not grow weary of doing good, for in due season we will reap, if we do not give up." (Galatians 6:9, ESV)

I don't know about you, but sometimes—no, often—I am *weary*. Up at 6 a.m. and running, my day of meetings, phone calls, schedule scrambling, basketball practice, homework, and dinner prep leave me exhausted, with just enough energy to crawl into bed around midnight. The verse above makes me feel…disheartened. I just don't have *time* to do good.

Kim, a friend of mine at work, is amazing. She's right there with me in the constant go-go-go, yet somehow she *does* find time to do good (often *for me*). Anytime someone needs a meal or a ride to work or help moving, she somehow fits it into her day. How does she manage it all, and why can't I be more that way? Am I just not diligent with my time? Does she have more energy than I do or just more passion and determination? Embarrassed as I am to admit it, while people who do good inspire me, they bum me out too; observing their good deeds makes me feel disheartened. I just don't have the energy to "do good."

The other day I rushed out of the grocery store with my 9-year-old in tow, his hot chocolate sloshing as we hurried. A man stood in the cold, ringing a bell for the Salvation Army kettle. He sang out "Merry Christmas" and flashed us an infectious grin. His clothes were bedraggled and worn, his whiskers a bit long, his coat not warm enough to insulate against the December chill. As I dashed by, I mumbled an apology for never having cash and always using my debit card.

"Mommy," my son said, tugging at my arm. "That man looks cold. Can we buy him a hot cocoa like mine?" What could I say? We went back and got the man a hot cocoa. As Jack handed him the cup, I smiled and said, "You look cold! God bless!"

On the way home, Jack and I talked about what a great feeling it is being able to give, to brighten someone's day. Five minutes for a hot cocoa. That's not bad—I can handle that. Rather than sapping the little energy I had, this "doing good" thing filled me with joy and put a smile on my face.

I don't want to give up! Maybe doing good is a muscle. Maybe that's how Kim gets the energy and finds the time. She started out with smaller, lighter lifting and worked her way up to the heavier stuff.

Amy Taylor

Close your eyes…take a deep breath and pray: "Lord, I don't want to grow weary of doing good. Today, as I rush around in my busyness, please bring to my attention one small thing that I can do to bless someone. Thank you. In Jesus' name. Amen."

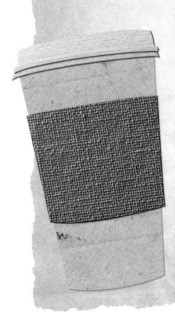

Declutter Your *Life*

Connecting Together

Clutter Continuums

Discuss:

• What did your upbringing teach you about clutter?

_____

_____

_____

Minimalist.. Maximalist

Connecting to the Topic

Discuss:

• If someone were to poke around the place you keep things
  that you don't use—but won't get rid of—who would they think
  you are based on what they find?

_____

_____

_____

_____

Conquering Clutter:
Tips From Gretchen Rubin

1. Choose to value clearing clutter—most people find it energizing even as it leads to inner calm.

2. Get rid of what's out of date, no longer used, or broken.

3. Be wary of accepting free items; they often become clutter.

4. Stop clutter before it follows you home. Before making a purchase, ask, "Where will I put this? Will I *really* use it?"

5. Before a clothing purchase, ask, "Will I wear this tomorrow?"

6. Make purchases that reflect your real life, not your fantasy life.

7. One-Minute Declutter Rule: If you can do it in a minute, do it. Small tasks pile up and become overwhelming.

8. Fifteen-Minute Declutter Rule: Set a timer and jump into a hard job—but for just 15 minutes. Just 15 minutes per day makes a serious dent in clutter.

9. Get to know yourself so you can use your time, energy, and money in the ways that let you be true to yourself.

10. Evaluate your space: Does it reflect what's important to you?

11. Consider your use of time: Why do you do what you do? Are you spending time with the people and activities that matter most to you?

12. If it's important, get it on your schedule.

13. Treat yourself like a toddler.

Discuss:

• Which of these tips would you like to try—and why?

_____

_____

_____

Other Clutter-Cutting Ideas:

Connecting With God

"I've been surprised how much, in most people, outer order contributes to inner calm." —Gretchen Rubin

A recent survey of more than 20,000 Christians from around the world found that nearly 60 percent say they're too busy to develop a deeper relationship with God.

Discuss:

• How might some of Gretchen's tips apply to decluttering your spiritual life?

Schedule it!

_____

_____

• What have you found that works for you to make room for God in your life?

_____

_____

_____

Connecting to My Life

"The news about Jesus spread even more. Many people came to hear Jesus and to be healed of their sicknesses, but Jesus often slipped away to be alone so he could pray." (Luke 5:15-16, NCV)

My location:

Kitchen Table

My day/time:

after everyone has gone to bed.

Credit Card Tip

Cut out this card below and tuck it next to your credit cards. The next time you pull out your plastic, ask yourself these three questions. Maybe you'll prevent some clutter from following you home.

Additional Thoughts on Decluttering Your Life

Relationships take time. I hate to make phone calls because of the time it takes away from other things I should be doing. My friend Kris often calls me to go and get coffee with her. I will put her off for weeks before her nagging makes me give in. When we do meet up, it is always delightful, but we end up talking for more than two hours and I go home with a caffeine buzz and a guilt trip. I stress that I didn't get the really important things done, the things that people will notice like laundry and grocery shopping and picking up the stuff that needs to be put in its place. Those are the things that must be done or my family won't have food to eat or clothes to wear and none of us will be able to find what we need. I can put off talking with a friend and life will still go on smoothly. Kris will wait.

I have another friend, Jana, who likes to drop by and insist we walk and talk. She knows me well enough to know that I also put off exercise. We end up chatting and strolling until our feet hurt and our hearts are full. We are proud of ourselves that we can check exercising off our list and can justify our time together. Funny, I rarely stress when I don't check off "call mom" or "write a letter to your sister" from my to-do list. It can always be done tomorrow.

The other day the radio DJ posed the question, "What would you do if you knew it was your last day on earth?" My answer was that I would want to tell all my friends and family how much I loved them. Would I have enough time then? I got to thinking about how when Jesus was on earth he was all about relationships. In fact, I couldn't think of any Scriptures where he said, "I don't have time to talk to you now. I have more important things to do." Tending to relationships was top on his list.

Even when on the cross, Jesus spent some of his last few painful breaths to assure the man hanging next to him, "Today you will be with me in paradise." I looked up those words in Luke 23:43 to read them again. Jesus could have said, "Today you will be in paradise." Shouldn't that have been the most important thing to the man, knowing where he would spend eternity? Apparently not. Jesus showed us the true priority when he included the words "with me."

I think I'll call Kris and set up a coffee date.

Lindy Schneider

Get away from the clutter of busyness and act on what's most important. Make that phone call or send an email you've been putting off. Let someone know that they matter to you. The laundry will wait.

Handling Stress

Connecting Together

Discuss:

• If you could get rid of just one chore or responsibility that is currently on your plate, what would you choose?

_____

_____

_____

_____

• If you could give up not just one chore for a day, but could give up every responsibility for one day, and money was not a limiting factor, how would you spend your day?

_____

_____

_____

_____

Connecting to the Topic

Discuss:

• Is the stress I feel today caused more be internal or external factors? Share with your group why you've answered this way.

_____

_____

_____

_____

Connecting With God

In Matthew 6:26-27, Jesus says, "Look at the birds. They don't plant or harvest or store food in barns, for your heavenly Father feeds them. And aren't you far more valuable to him than they are? Can all your worries add a single moment to your life?"

Discuss:

• How would you answer the questions that Jesus asked?

_____

_____

_____

_____

• What does this verse help you realize about all the stresses in your life?

_____

_____

_____

_____

Psalm 55:22 tells us to "Give your burdens to the Lord, and he will take care of you. He will not permit the godly to slip and fall."

- What makes giving your burdens to God a challenge for you? Or is it easy for you? If so, share how you do this with the moms in your group.

_____

_____

_____

_____

Matthew 11:28-30 says, "Then Jesus said, 'Come to me, all of you who are weary and carry heavy burdens, and I will give you rest. Take my yoke upon you. Let me teach you, because I am humble and gentle at heart, and you will find rest for your souls. For my yoke is easy to bear, and the burden I give you is light.'"

- What does this verse mean to you? How do you put it into practice in everyday terms?

_____

_____

_____

_____

My Plate

This stuff on my plate is causing me stress.

God's Plate

These are the things I can move off my plate and put on God's plate.

Connecting to My Life

"And now, dear brothers and sisters, one final thing. Fix your thoughts on what is true, and honorable, and right, and pure, and lovely, and admirable. Think about things that are excellent and worthy of praise." (Philippians 4:8)

• What might change in my stress levels if I followed the directions of this verse?

_____

_____

_____

• What's one way I can put the instructions of this verse into practice today?

_____

_____

_____

Additional Thoughts on Handling Stress

"We can make our plans, but the Lord determines our steps." (Proverbs 16:9)

As I sat down one morning with my Bible, coffee, and a desire to have my heart and mind totally fixed on the Lord and his truths, I was bombarded on all sides with thoughts of what the day held. Responsibilities and the urgency of what needed to be accomplished called for my attention. I knew I had better write these things down now or I may forget; but if I got up to get paper, I would surely get further distracted and feel a need to throw a load in the washer, tidy the counter, or sort a stack of paperwork. So I grabbed a 9-inch paper plate that happened to be within reach.

As I jotted down my to-do list for the day in order to clear my mind, I saw the plate was much too full, and I became overwhelmed. Then I remembered something my grandmother had told me many years before. She said, "Honey, if there needed to be more hours in the day, the good Lord would have given them to us. Everyone has 24 hours, and we each make the choice of how to spend them." She expressed a simple truth that was an "aha" moment for me. I had bought into the lie that there were not enough hours in the day.

As I reflected on the wisdom she expressed, I took my plate, which included all my plans written down the middle and around the sides, lifted it up, and prayed: "Lord, I give you this day and all of my plans of what seems so important. Clarify what of this is for me today, what is for another day, and what is not intended to be on my plate at all. Help me to differentiate between what is important and what is not—what has eternal implications and what is temporal."

Now I often intentionally make my to-do list on a paper plate and have at times considered getting a bigger plate (or even a platter) or writing smaller, but more often than not, as I commit myself and my plans to God, he provides clarity and encouragement and has been known to reduce my list to fit on a 6-inch dessert plate. He also reminds me that he wants me to make him my priority, and as I set my heart and thoughts accordingly, he enables me to accomplish more in less time.

Jennifer Sorcinelli

Jot down your to-do list on a 9-inch paper plate and lift it up with both hands. Pray something like, "Lord, I offer you myself, this plate, and everything on it. Help me differentiate between what is of you and what is not. Thank you that your yoke is easy and your burden is light."

The *Blessing* of *Sleep*
and How to Get Some!

Connecting Together

"If people were meant to pop out of bed, we'd all sleep in toasters." —Jim Davis

"There will be plenty of time to sleep once you are dead." —Ben Franklin

"Never under any circumstances take a sleeping pill and a laxative on the same night." —Dave Barry

Discuss:

• What sort of sleeper are you?

_____

_____

Connecting to the Topic

Discuss:

• Tell about a time in your life when you couldn't sleep. What kept you from sleeping?

_____

_____

_____

Three Myths About Sleep

1. We should all sleep soundly throughout the night.

2. We should fall asleep and wake up instantly.

3. Sleep medications help us have deeper, more restorative sleep.

• Which—if any—of these myths surprises you? And why?

_____

_____

_____

Connecting to My Life

Sleep Advantages

1. Physically restoring

2. Decelerates aging

3. Strengthens memory

4. Emotionally healing/recharging

5. Improves relationships

6. Enhances spiritual guidance

Discuss:

• Which of these benefits might prompt you to go to bed 20 minutes earlier tonight?

_____

_____

• Why does that benefit matter to you?

_____

_____

Suggestions for a Good Night's Sleep

Left untreated, chronic sleeplessness can lead to obesity, lethargy, and strained relationships. Try these practical tips for getting the sleep you need.

1. Darken the room.

Soften the lighting in your bedroom, and lessen your exposure to bright lights and screens as bedtime draws near.

2. Soften sounds.

Use a white noise machine or fan to cover sudden or unexpected sounds that might awaken you. Or try earplugs.

3. Adjust the temperature.

Cool, but not cold—comfort is key.

4. Gradually wind down.

Allow time to reflect on the day.

5. Reduce anxiety.

Jot a list of to-do's and what's bothering you so you can dismiss those thoughts from your mind.

6. Curtail caffeine.

Caffeine induces wakefulness and stays in your body up to seven hours.

7. Develop a ritual.

Lower the lights…enjoy a hot bath…light a candle…read a calming novel…pause to pray. In time, rituals can train your body to ease toward sleep.

8. Exercise daily.

An exercise routine helps you sleep. Just be sure to not exercise within three hours of your bedtime.

9. Find out if there's a deeper issue.

A chronic inability to sleep might have an underlying medical cause. If sleeplessness persists, contact your doctor.

A sleep suggestion I'd like to try:

_____

Other Sleep Tips:

Discuss:

• What's causing you anxiety these days? What's keeping you up at night?

_____

_____

_____

_____

_____

_____

Connecting With God

"Don't worry about anything; instead, pray about everything. Tell God what you need, and thank him for all he had done. Then you will experience God's peace, which exceeds anything we can understand." (Philippians 4:6-7)

Additional Thoughts on Getting Sleep

If you need more help, check out these websites.

SleepFoundation.org—The National Sleep Foundation promotes healthy sleep and provides data and helpful information.

SleepApnea.org—Online help determining if you might have sleep apnea and what steps to take if you fit the profile.

BetterSleep.org—Mattress makers uncover everything you've ever wanted to know about selecting the right mattress for a good night's sleep.

WorldSleepDay.org—Expert advice about sleep, video interviews with medical providers, and written resources.

Notes

_____

_____

_____

_____

_____

_____

_____

_____

_____

Notes

_____

_____

_____

_____

_____

_____

_____

_____

_____

_____

_____

_____

_____

_____

_____

_____

Lord, Give Me Patience—
Quickly!

Connecting Together

I find myself losing patience when…

_____

_____

Connecting to the Topic

With your group read each scenario and determine what we teach our children by these actions. Jot down your thoughts so you can share them with others later.

- You're on the phone and your child keeps pulling on your arm and interrupting. In frustration you snap a sharp answer to your child.

_____

_____

- The line at the grocery store is five people deep, each with a full grocery cart. You and your kids wait, but you grumble the entire time and make a snarky remark to the cashier about the time you had to wait.

_____

_____

- When ordering online you notice that for only an additional $5.00 you can get faster delivery. Not wanting to wait an extra few days, you pay the additional money for faster delivery.

_____

_____

- At a restaurant your service isn't as quick as you would like. You make a few comments to your kids that you know the staff can hear and leave a less than fair tip.

_____

_____

- While at the mall the people in front of you are walking far too slowly. With a loud and exaggerated sigh you race around them and hurry to the next store.

_____

_____

- A friend is taking far too long to tell what should be a short story. You cut her off and say, "That's some story! I'll sure be praying for you."

_____

_____

Connecting With God

One woman can read this verse aloud to the table group:

"A person's wisdom yields patience; it is to one's glory to overlook an offense." (Proverbs 19:11, NIV)

Discuss:

- Why does wisdom yield patience?

_____

_____

- In what ways does patience bring "glory" or credit to someone?

_____

_____

- How might overlooking "an offense" of your child be beneficial to them and you?

_____

_____

Have one mom read this verse:

"A hot-tempered person stirs up conflict, but the one who is patient calms a quarrel." (Proverbs 15:18, NIV)

- How have you seen the truth of this verse in your own family?

_____

_____

Have one mom read this verse:

"Therefore, as God's chosen people, holy and dearly loved, clothe yourselves with compassion, kindness, humility, gentleness and patience." (Colossians 3:12, NIV)

- Is patience something God gives us or a choice we make? Explain your answer.

_____

_____

Connecting to My Life

Tips or methods that can help me choose patience:

_____

_____

_____

_____

_____

_____

_____

_____

Discuss:

• Reread the scenarios in the "Connecting to the Topic" section. How could you respond in patience, and what would your response teach your children?

_____

_____

_____

_____

_____

_____

_____

_____

Additional Thoughts on Patience

Slow down.

Take a deep breath.

Count to ten.

Learning patience isn't always easy. It takes, well, patience. And it's possibly why they say it's a virtue...because not everyone will see the wisdom of embracing a practice that seems to deny your own emotions and desires. Especially in our fast-paced, rights-centered culture. But did you know that by practicing patience you are displaying God? It's true.

The Hebrew word for patience in the Old Testament is *arek*. This word is sometimes translated as "patience" or "longsuffering," but often it is translated as "slow to anger." You may recognize this as a common descriptor of God:

> *"The Lord is gracious and merciful, slow to anger and abounding in steadfast love."* (Psalm 145:8, NIV)

> *"They refused to listen and failed to remember the miracles you performed among them. They became stiff-necked and in their rebellion appointed a leader in order to return to their slavery. But you are a forgiving God, gracious and compassionate, slow to anger and abounding in love. Therefore you did not desert them."* (Nehemiah 9:16-17, NIV)

> *"Rend your heart and not your garments. Return to the Lord your God, for he is gracious and compassionate, slow to anger and abounding in love, and he relents from sending calamity."* (Joel 2:13, NIV)

All of these verses say the same thing...God is slow to anger. He is patient and abounding in love. Take a few minutes to take that in and realize God is patient with you. He is abounding in love toward you. It's pretty amazing, really.

In the New Testament we also see that God is patient, but we also read that we are to be like him.

"Imitate God, therefore, in everything you do, because you are his dear children. Live a life filled with love, following the example of Christ. He loved us and offered himself as a sacrifice for us, a pleasing aroma to God." (Ephesians 5:1-2)

"May God, who gives this patience and encouragement, help you live in complete harmony with each other, as is fitting for followers of Christ Jesus." (Romans 15:5)

If you look at your own life, you see God's patience. He bears with sinning and stubbornness and willfulness and "abounds in love" toward you. He is "slow to anger." The character of God is so marked by patience that in Romans 15 Paul gives him the title "God of patience." He wants our character to be marked by patience as well so that as we interact with our kids, deal with customers, or interact with the cashier at the store, we will display the same forgiving, gracious, patient, and loving attitude as our Lord.

How will you display God's patient love today?

Notes

_____

_____

_____

_____

_____

_____

_____

Overcoming *Worry*

Connecting Together

What did you worry about when you were a child?

_____

_____

_____

_____

Connecting to the Topic

Worry Versus Anxiety

Definition of Worry:

To worry is to give way to anxiety or unease, to allow one's mind to dwell on difficulty or troubles.

Discuss:

• What's a big worry you're facing?

_____

_____

_____

_____

Ramifications of Worry

- Worry triggers your body's "flight or fight" response, the response that's designed to get you out of trouble and releases stress hormones into your system to deal with the stress.

- These hormones can cause physical symptoms like headaches, dizziness, aches and pains, nausea, and sweating.

- If your body doesn't burn off these additional stress hormones, they can suppress your immune system and create more severe symptoms like digestive problems.

- If worry continues to go untreated, it can turn into depression and suicidal thoughts and even trigger a heart attack.

Under Control

A few ways to control worry:

- **Use the 50-year rule.** Ask yourself, "Will this matter in 50 years? Is what I'm worrying about really so important? Just how much is this worry worth?"

- **Exercise.** Exercise can change your brain chemistry and reduce excessive worrying.

- **Turn worries into plans and actions.** Worry is only constructive when it spurs you to approach and tackle problems.

- **Talk to people who can listen and give wise advice.** Hopefully you can find some of those people here at Where Moms Connect.

- **Pray.** God listens.

- **Get enough rest and sleep.** Fatigue contributes to worrying.

- **Try to stay focused on the present.** Most of us live in the past and future. But it's hard to worry when you're living in and appreciating the present moment.

- **Maintain perspective.** When your mood is low, your outlook will be pessimistic. Remember that your down mood is not the truth, but only one view of reality.

- **Accept that you will never get everything done.** You may come close, but there will always be more to do.

- **Simply drop or cut loose your worry.** Make a decision to let it go.

Other ideas I want to remember:

_____

_____

_____

_____

Quotes From Cheryl Eresman

"It's almost always worse in your head than it is in reality."

"Your worry doesn't change anything."

"Jesus said, 'Do not worry about tomorrow because tomorrow will take care of itself.'"

Discuss:

- Which of these quotes resonates with you most? Why?

_____

_____

_____

Maintaining Perspective

Discuss:

- Tell about a time you were consumed with worry. What was the outcome?

_____

_____

_____

Connecting With God

"Do not be anxious about anything, but in every situation, by prayer and petition, with thanksgiving, present your requests to God. And the peace of God, which transcends all understanding, will guard your hearts and your minds in Christ Jesus." (Philippians 4:6-7, NIV)

Connecting to My Life

My prayer:

_____

_____

_____

_____

_____

_____

_____

_____

_____

_____

_____

_____

_____

_____

Additional Thoughts on Overcoming Worry

"This is my command—be strong and courageous! Do not be afraid or discouraged. For the Lord your God is with you wherever you go." (Joshua 1:9)

I'm not exactly a brave person. In fact, being a worrier is what I'm known for among my friends and family. They always seem quite amused at whatever my latest worry is. For example, a huge fear of mine at the moment is being attacked by bats while I sleep. I grew up in a house with bats in the attic...so I'm sure it isn't exactly out of the realm of possibility.

All jokes aside, fear and worry are the biggest struggles for me in my Christian walk. Worry over life at the moment, worry for the future, worry about when I'm supposed to step out in faith, worry if I'm following God as he is leading me or not. I *know* I am to trust God and that he will protect me. It's his promise. But it's still not easy for me.

One of the roles I've been blessed with over the years is being a Sunday school teacher to preschoolers. In a recent lesson, the children were memorizing Joshua 1:9. In my lesson prep, the actual words of the verse didn't really stand out to me.

On that Sunday morning, I was struck at the irony of *me* teaching about trusting God. We practiced the words to the verse and added some fun hand motions. We started by saying the verse as softly as we could and then we gradually grew louder as I shouted, "Say it louder now!"

I was brought to tears as I watched Kenzie, Mason, Cameron, Jaxon, and the rest of their 3-year-old classmates shout as loudly as they could how God is with them all the time. Later when we were discussing the different circumstances in which God is with us, I had quite a chuckle hearing their examples (you can use your imagination!).

In that moment for those 3-year-olds, the thought of God being everywhere was enough. It filled them with joy and excitement. They weren't asking questions or doubting. God is the friend who doesn't have to leave and go home.

Later as I was cleaning up the crushed cheerios on the floor, I realized I should have the same exuberance over God's presence in my life. I truly don't have to fear because he is with me always.

God puts all kinds of people in our lives to inspire us and remind us of what's important. That Sunday, those fifteen 3-year-olds spoke more truth into my life than they could have ever realized. They reminded me it's okay to trust God without hesitation or fear.

Jessica Burkell

Notes

_____

_____

_____

_____

_____

_____

_____

_____

Stay at Home or Have a Career—
What's a Mom to Do?

Connecting Together

Discuss:

• If you could have any job or career in the world, what would it be?

_____

_____

_____

_____

_____

_____

Connecting to the Topic

There are many different seasons of life and jobs to do in each season. Whether you are in a season of staying home with small children or chauffeuring older kids or whether this season finds you leaving the house each day to work in an office, the important thing is to try to operate within your gifts and your calling and to remember how blessed you are so that you can be a blessing! Discuss these questions with your partner or partners.

"Home" Moms

- What are a few of the best things about being home with your kids?

_____

_____

- What are a few of the hardest things about being at home?

_____

_____

- What two things do you wish you could change about your situation?

_____

_____

- What are two ways you can bless or encourage a mom who works outside the home?

_____

_____

"Career" Moms

- What are a few of the best things about your job?

_____

_____

- What are a few of the hardest things about being in the workplace?

_____

_____

- What two things do you wish you could change about your situation?

_____

_____

- What are two ways you can bless or encourage a mom who stays at home with her family?

_____

_____

"Both" Moms

- What are a few of the things you like best about working from your home?

_____

_____

- Where are a few of the hardest things about doing both?

_____

_____

- What two things do you wish you could change about your situation?

_____

_____

- What are two ways you can bless or encourage a mom who has chosen a different path than you?

_____

_____

Connecting With God

Did you know that women in the Bible worked a variety of jobs? It's true. The Bible mentions Lydia as a merchant of expensive cloth (Acts 16:14), Priscilla as a tentmaker (Acts 18:3), and Ephraim's granddaughter Sheerah as a builder of towns (1 Chronicles 7:23-24). Women also worked in agriculture and as nurses, traders, artisans, perfumers, and cooks. In the book of Judges, Deborah had one of the highest positions in the land as a prophetess and judge of Israel (Judges 4:4).

Women also have important work to do with their families at home. Read the following verses aloud around your table and discuss the questions below.

"And you must commit yourselves wholeheartedly to these commands that I am giving you today. Repeat them again and again to your children. Talk about them when you are at home and when you are on the road, when you are going to bed and when you are getting up." (Deuteronomy 6:6-7)

"Direct your children onto the right path, and when they are older, they will not leave it." (Proverbs 22:6)

"But watch out! Be careful never to forget what you yourself have seen. Do not let these memories escape from your mind as long as you live! And be sure to pass them on to your children and grandchildren." (Deuteronomy 4:9)

- Whether you are home or in the workplace, how are you following God's instructions for your family?

_____

_____

- When the Bible demonstrates that there are moms who were very like moms today—some with careers and some without—why do you think we are so judgmental toward moms who have made a choice different from our own?

_____

_____

Connecting to My Life

- Write a note to yourself, affirming the choice you have made. Remember the reasons you're in this season of life, and remind yourself that you are where God wants you to be.

_____

_____

_____

_____

- What's one way you will affirm another mom this week— specifically a mom who has made a choice that is different from your own?

_____

_____

_____

_____

Additional Thoughts on Staying Home or Having a Career

In order to do our jobs with excellence and to be a blessing, we need to recharge our batteries. This week try a few of these ideas to bring new energy to your life:

- Read a few Bible verses. The psalms are great for short reads with great encouragement.

- Listen to an audio version of the Bible. Easy if you need to keep your hands free for folding laundry or driving.

- Pray in the shower or in your car (Keep your eyes open if you're driving! ☺)

- Do something nice for yourself. A nap is a good start!

- Take a walk outside at lunch time.

- Enjoy a hot bath.

- Write yourself a note of encouragement and put it on your bathroom mirror.

Also, think of ways you can partner with other moms to lighten each other's loads. If you stay home, could you help by making dinner for a working mom? If you work, could you encourage a stay-at-home mom by giving her a call on your lunch break so she could hear another adult's voice during her day? We are better moms when we work together.

Notes

_____

_____

_____

_____

_____

_____

_____

_____

_____

_____

Keeping Love Alive

Connecting Together

Discuss:

• Tell about an actual storm you've experienced. What made it so memorable?

_____

_____

I want to keep this person in my life because...

_____

_____

Connecting to the Topic

Discuss:

- Lisa said that there came a time when the wedding ring stayed on but the engagement ring came off. She loved John, but she didn't like him.

  What's the difference between like and love—especially in a marriage?

  _____

  _____

  _____

- Tell about a loving relationship that started out strong but faded away. What happened?

  _____

  _____

  _____

The Loss of Love

According to the National Fatherhood Initiative, relationships fail due to the following reasons:

- A lack of commitment

- Arguing and poor communication

- Infidelity and loss of trust

- Unrealistic expectations

- Inequality

- Insufficient preparation

- Abuse

Weathering Relationship Storms

Discuss:

- What might we learn from John and Lisa about keeping love alive?

_____

_____

_____

Tips:

- Marry a similar spender.

- Accept.

- Say "thank you" and "we."

- Have novel experiences.

- Work at it.

Advice From John and Lisa:

- Talk. Connect and communicate.

- Honor your commitment.

- Demonstrate your love in observable ways.

- Choose to love—even if you don't like the person at the moment.

- Care for others even when they're not at their best.

- Hold hands.

- Say, "I love you." Saying it helps you feel it.

- Open up—share what you're really thinking and feeling.

- Pray for each other.

- Invite God into your relationship.

More ideas:

_____

_____

_____

_____

_____

_____

Connecting to My Life

Discuss:

• Which of these ideas would you like to try as you seek to strengthen the relationship represented by your heart?

_____

_____

_____

• What do you expect the response to be?

_____

_____

_____

Connecting With God

"Love one another. In the same way I loved you, you love one another." (John 13:34, _The Message_)

Additional Thoughts on Keeping Love Alive

Want to keep love alive? Here are fun ideas you can do with just about anyone—a family member, your spouse, or a friend. Try one or more of these ideas:

- Be kind. For a whole day, speak only words that are kind and loving. Don't allow even one criticism or sarcastic comment to slip in.

- Ask, "How can I make your life better today?" and then do it! Variations on this are "How can I brighten your day today?" or "What could I do to help you today?"

- Listen. Without interrupting, rolling your eyes, or giving advice. Just listen.

- Take a picture of the two of you together. Post it on your favorite social media site with a note declaring how much you love, like, or care about this person.

- Tuck a note somewhere. Lunchbox, purse, backpack, under a pillow, taped to the steering wheel of the car, or wherever it will be found later. Just remind that person you think he or she is amazing.

- Send a note or greeting card in the mail. Yes, the old-fashioned mail. Since it hardly ever gets used anymore, it makes your note all the more special!

- Leave flowers. They're not just for girls. Some guys like them too! Or wrap bacon around a flower to leave for a guy. ☺

- Do a small task you know that person hates doing. Fold the laundry or take out the trash or wash the dishes.

Notes

_____

_____

_____

_____

_____

_____

_____

_____

_____

_____

_____

_____

_____

_____

_____

_____

_____

How to *Trust God* With *Your Children*

Connecting Together

Discuss:

• What's the most valuable thing you own? And why does it have such a high value to you?

_____

_____

Holding On to What's Valuable

Discuss:

• As you see your own valuable item in someone else's hands, honestly say how long you would be comfortable leaving that item in this other person's care. A minute? An hour? A few days? What amount of time would you be comfortable leaving that item in her hands?

_____

_____

• How do you feel about the responsibility of what has been placed in your hands by another mom? Are you comfortable taking her valuable item into your care or not? Explain your answer.

_____

_____

Before I Trust You...

If you were to put that valuable item into the hands of someone else, you'd have questions you would want answered before you let go. Here are a few you might want answered.

- What are they going to do with my valuable item?

- Is this person trustworthy?

- Does this person know how important this item is? Do they understand its value?

- Where are they going to keep it?

- Will they misuse it?

What are other questions you would want answered before you handed over that item?

_____

_____

_____

_____

Connecting to the Topic

Out of My Hands

- What are some of the moments when you are very aware that your child is taking a step away from you and is in the hands of someone else?

_____

_____

_____

_____

Letting Go

Look back at the list from the "Out of My Hands" section. Choose one of the situations that you wrote that also has a name next to it. Then keep that in mind as you discuss these questions with your group:

- As you see your own valuable child in someone else's hands, honestly say how long you are comfortable leaving your child in this other person's care and in that specific situation. A minute? An hour? A few days? What amount of time would you be comfortable leaving your child in this person's hands?

_____

_____

_____

- What's the difference between placing an item of value and a child of value into the hands of someone else? How do your feelings change, and why?

_____

_____

_____

Connecting With God

Discuss:

- What is one way you are currently struggling with the idea of putting your child or children into God's hands? Share with your group about something that's happening in your life now.

_____

_____

_____

Keep these situations in mind as you read through the following Bible verses and discuss the questions that follow them.

"If you need wisdom, ask our generous God, and he will give it to you. He will not rebuke you for asking." (James 1:5)

• As you think of the current situation you described above, where do you need wisdom?

_____

_____

_____

After each mom has shared, stop right now and pray for each other. Ask God for wisdom.

Read Psalm 139:16:

"You saw me before I was born. Every day of my life was recorded in your book. Every moment was laid out before a single day had passed."

• God created your child and knows every moment of your child's life. How might this truth help you trust God with what's ahead for your child?

_____

_____

_____

Connecting to My Life

Philippians 4:6-7 says:

"Don't worry about anything; instead, pray about everything. Tell God what you need, and thank him for all he has done. Then you will experience God's peace, which exceeds anything we can understand. His peace will guard your hearts and minds as you live in Christ Jesus."

• Tell God what you need. Write that here.

_____

_____

_____

_____

• Thank God for all he has done. Write that here.

_____

_____

_____

_____

• Quiet your heart. Wait for God's peace.

Additional Thoughts on How to Trust God With Your Children

"Every word of God proves true. He is a shield to all who come to him for protection." (Proverbs 30:5)

From the moment our children are born, our instinct is to protect them. We want the best for them. We want to shield them from the cruelties of the world. We want to wrap them in a blanket and swaddle them and keep them close forever. Yet as they grow older, we know we have to loosen that blanket and let them become the people God intended.

As soon as I knew I was expecting until this very day, I have been quilting a blanket of prayer for each of my children. I know God loves them even more than I ever could. Thus, I know my prayers for protection and guidance will not be in vain.

One of my sons taught me how precious prayer is for him and the peace it can bring. As a captain in the Army, his unit was being sent overseas, off to war. I have no words to describe the fear I had. If I could, I would have gladly gone in his place. This mommy wanted her boy home on friendly soil. As he prepared to leave, I realized the best thing I could do for him was pray. A good friend reminded me that the same God who was protecting him here at home would protect him no matter where he was in the world. The peace those words gave me is immeasurable.

Of course, every time I heard a news report of a young man losing his life or being injured, I wept, but I also gave thanks that it was not my son whose name was reported in the newspaper. Prayer is what kept me going, and my son told me more times than I can count how he felt the prayers so many were extending on his behalf.

Whether your child is heading off to his first sleepover, off to college, or off to war, wrap your child in a blanket of prayer. The peace it brings will change both your lives.

You might want to start a prayer journal for your child. Record your prayers and praises for him or her. Keep a record of the things God has done for your child through prayer.

Jennifer Nystrom

Understanding and Supporting People
Dealing With Mental Illness

Connecting Together

Discuss:

- Tell the moms at your table about something you—or a person you know—cherished as a child.

Connecting to the Topic

Definition of Mental Health

Mental illness is a medical condition that disrupts a person's thinking, feeling, moods, ability to relate to others, and daily function.

The National Institute of Health reports:

- 1 in 4 adults experiences a mental health disorder in any given year.

The World Health Organization reports:

- 4 of the 10 leading causes of disability in developed countries are mental disorders.

- By 2020, depression will be the leading cause of disability for women and children.

- Of the people suffering with a diagnosable mental disorder, only 1 in 3 will seek treatment.

Discuss:

- How do you know when someone is mentally ill? And what—if anything—should you do if you have suspicions?

_____

_____

_____

Symptoms of Mental Illness

Symptoms vary, but the following are common signs of major mental illnesses. Experiencing these symptoms doesn't mean someone is mentally ill, but a person experiencing them might benefit from seeing a health care professional.

- Sudden mood swings

- Confusion

- Diminished concentration

- Lingering sadness and depression

- Sleeping too much or too little

- Chronic fatigue and lack of energy

- Inattention to personal appearance and hygiene

- Withdrawal from previously enjoyed activities

- A lack of ability to deal with everyday challenges

- Unexplained back pain, headaches, and stomachaches

- Emotional highs and lows, or extreme spikes of anger

- Extreme anxiety and worry

- Substance abuse—food, drugs, alcohol, or other substances

- Hallucinations

- Suicidal thoughts

Who's Story

When you think of Amy's story, who in that story do you identify with the most—and why?

- Amy

- Her dad

- The receptionist

- The people in the waiting room

- Amy's mother

Connecting With God

Discuss:

- Amy's take on suffering and illness—including mental illness— isn't that God is punishing us. Rather, it's the result of sin, of our living in a fallen and broken world.

  Do you agree or disagree with Amy's viewpoint? Share why.

  _____

  _____

  _____

  _____

"You will know the truth, and the truth will set you free."
—Jesus (John 8:32)

Additional Thoughts on Mental Illness

If you need additional information or help, here are a few resources for you:

Nami.org—The National Alliance on Mental Illness provides links to local chapters, as well as information regarding research and treatment.

MentalHealthAmerica.net—Mental Health America provides practical help with finding support and treatment, as well as tips for choosing and paying for treatment.

If there are suicidal thoughts...

• Call 911 immediately, or

• Call 800-273-TALK (800-273-8255) to be routed to a counselor

If someone in your life is losing control...

If someone threatens harm to himself or others, or plans to break a law, call 911 immediately.

And no matter what, lean on God...

You're not alone in your pain. Echo the thoughts of David, a Bible writer, who wrote:

"Be merciful to me, O God, be merciful to me, for in you my soul takes refuge; in the shadow of your wings I will take refuge, until the destroying storms pass by." (Psalm 57:1, NRS)

The Family That
Plays Together
Stays Together

Connecting Together

Discuss:

• What's your earliest happy, playful memory?

_____

_____

_____

_____

Connecting to the Topic

The Benefits of Laughter

Physical Benefits of Laughter

- Boosts immune system

- Lowers stress

- Decreases pain

- Relaxes muscles

- Prevents heart disease

Mental Benefits of Laughter

- Adds joy and zest to life

- Eases anxiety and fear

- Relieves stress

- Improves mood

- Enhances resilience

Social Benefits of Laughter (Keep in mind that your family is one of your social groups.)

- Strengthens relationships

- Attracts others to us

- Enhances team work

- Helps diffuse conflict

- Promotes group bonding

Discuss:

- Share about a time when your family experienced laughter and how that experience positively impacted your family.

_____

_____

_____

_____

_____

_____

Family Play Ideas

- Go on a family photo safari around your neighborhood. Take pictures of animals or insects you see.

- Family recess! Set a time when the whole family will take a 15-minute break from whatever they are doing and play! You may have to blow a whistle and set a timer but just do it. (Depending on the weather and age of children, find activities to get everyone moving such as foursquare, dodge ball, jump rope, a quick card game, or hide and seek.)

- Paint by number

- Charades

- Chopped. Hold your own family cooking contest!

- Sardines (Turn off all lights in the house. Then one person hides. The rest of the family wanders through the house seeking the hidden person. When they find him, they hide with that person until everyone is hiding and the last person finds the group. Ssshhhh, keep it quiet and dark.)

- Water fight!

- Board games are always a great option. Select a game appropriate for different ages. Teens love Settlers of Catan or Risk, for the little ones Chutes and Ladders or Candy Land. For all ages try Apples to Apples, or make Candy Land fun for the teens using real candy as rewards.

Now brainstorm some of your own ideas together. You might want to start with ideas for toddlers, then tweens and teens, then ideas for families with multiple ages of children. Jot your ideas here:

_____

_____

_____

_____

Connecting With God

One woman can read this verse aloud to the table group:

"A cheerful heart is good medicine, but a broken spirit saps a person's strength." (Proverbs 17:22)

• What does a "cheerful heart" look like to you?

_____

_____

_____

_____

• How can a cheerful heart be good medicine? Describe a time in your own life when you experienced this to be true.

_____

_____

_____

_____

• How does having a cheerful heart help develop playful times in our family lives?

_____

_____

_____

_____

Have one mom read this verse:

"A person standing alone can be attacked and defeated, but two can stand back-to-back and conquer. Three are even better, for a triple-braided cord is not easily broken." (Ecclesiastes 4:12)

- How do you think this verse relates to our topic today of a family who plays together stays together?

_____

_____

_____

_____

Connecting to My Life

First, write down what you think God would like you to take away from today's session.

_____

_____

_____

_____

Then consider a "game plan" to help your family get more excited about playing together. What will you do today or this week to help your family be more playful? Here are a few ideas:

- Ask your family for ideas on what they think would be fun play ideas together.
- Set a specific time to play.
- Play together! Just do it!
- Draw names to see who gets to plan the next family play time.

These are just a few ideas—what do you think will work best for your family?

_____

_____

_____

Additional Thoughts on Family Play

It's easy to talk about play, but how do you begin to do it more in everyday life? One idea is to start developing your own playful spirit. As moms we can get so serious about work, chores, school, and even sports. We can get so caught up in the daily grind we forget to have fun. We fall into bed exhausted and get up and do it all over again. So one suggestion to get you started is to learn to lighten up in your own life. Here are some ideas on how to begin:

- Don't take yourself so seriously. (It's okay if dinner is a little blackened.)

- Look for humor in situations. (You can call a blackened dinner "Cajun food" ☺.)

- Surround yourself with reminders to lighten up. (A toy on your desk or crayons and a coloring book.)

- Keep things in perspective. (Remember what you can and can't control.)

- Pay attention to children. They are experts at taking life lightly, laughing and playing. (Copy them!)

The Bible even talks about emulating children:

*"One day some parents brought their children to Jesus so he could touch and bless them. But the disciples scolded the parents for bothering him. When Jesus saw what was happening, he was angry with his disciples. He said to them, 'Let the children come to me. Don't stop them. **For the Kingdom of God belongs to those who are like these children.** I tell you the truth, anyone who does not receive the Kingdom of God like a child will never enter it.' Then he took the children in his arms and placed his hands on their heads and blessed them."* (Mark 10:13-16)

- When you think of little children, what characteristics do you think of?

_____

_____

_____

_____

- How can you emulate children today in your own life?

_____

_____

_____

_____

- If you have time this week, visit a playground and observe little children at play. Write down your observations.

_____

_____

_____

_____

- Try to adopt one childlike behavior this week and see if you find yourself laughing more or feeling more lighthearted. Write about that experience here.

_____

_____

_____

_____

- How can you be more childlike in your relationship with God? (Be ready to be blessed!)

_____

_____

_____

_____

As an influencer in your family culture, you can lead your family with a playful spirit. Once they see you playing and laughing more, they will too.

It's contagious!

Coping With
Food Allergies

Connecting Together

Discuss:

• Tell about a food you react to. What is it, and what's
your reaction?

_____

_____

_____

Poison Plate Review

• Do you, or someone you know, have any cause to be afraid
of what's on this plate? If so, why?

_____

_____

_____

Although nearly any food is capable of causing an allergic reaction, only eight foods account for 90 percent of all food-allergic reactions in the United States. These foods are:

- Peanuts

- Tree nuts

- Milk

- Egg

- Wheat

- Soy

- Fish

- Shellfish

Connecting to the Topic

In 1999, 3 to 4 percent of children had a food allergy. A study released in 2013 shows that 5.1 percent of children now have food allergies.

Discuss:

- What—if anything—did you hear that surprised you?

_____

_____

- Given what you heard about the rise in food allergies, what—if anything—should be done about it?

_____

_____

Invisible Pain

"It's not like a fever or broken bone that's visible...but it does affect my life." —Tricia Keefer

- Tell about a time you suffered with invisible pain. What was it, and how did people respond to you?

_____

_____

_____

"How much do I inflict my way of eating on others?"

Case Study

- Did the school do enough, or should more have been done? What should the school district pay, if anything?

_____

_____

_____

Connecting With God

Read the Scripture verse and discuss the questions below.

"Don't look out only for your own interests, but take an interest in others, too." (Philippians 2:4)

- In your life, how does that passage apply to you when you're dealing with people who have food allergies?

_____

_____

_____

- If you have a food allergy, how does that passage apply to you as you deal with those who do not have food allergies?

_____

_____

_____

Connecting to My Life

- Who in my life has a food allergy:

_____

_____

- What's one thing you can do this week for one person on your list to make them feel accepted and to help them cope?

_____

_____

Additional Thoughts on Coping With Food Allergies

Here are a few websites you might want to check out—and some recipes that were mentioned in our discussion this week!

FoodAllergy.org/allergens—General research and education information

KidsWithFoodAllergies.org—Links to support groups for parents and caregivers

aafa.org—Asthma and allergy support groups for adults

Tricia's Gluten-Free Pizza Crust

It looks complicated, but mostly it's just different. Try it. Experiment. And enjoy!

1. Grease four 12-inch baking sheets and preheat oven to 400 degrees.

2. Mix the following dry ingredients in the bowl of a heavy-duty mixer:

   2 cups brown rice flour

   2 cups tapioca flour

1 tablespoons xanthan gum

1½ teaspoons yeast

1 teaspoon to 1 tablespoon sugar or honey (optional)

1 teaspoon salt

½ teaspoon pepper

1½ teaspoon dried oregano

1½ teaspoon ground fennel seeds

3. Add the following ingredients to dry ingredients at low speed; then mix on high speed for 3 minutes:

4 egg whites

¼ cup oil

1½ cups hot water (Add more if needed, up to 2 cups. Dough will be soft, almost like a batter, and will stick to the sides of the bowl.)

4. Divide dough onto greased baking sheets, wetting your hands to flatten and spread the dough over the entire pan. Bake the crusts for 12 to 14 minutes.

5. Cool baked pizza crusts and freeze or spread with your favorite toppings and bake at 400 degrees for an additional 10 to 14 minutes.

Tips:

For individual crusts, use 6 or 7 cake pans. For a crowd, choose 1 or 2 large cookie sheets, depending on how thick you like your crust.

Brown rice flour is not sacred—you can replace it with a mix of other gluten-free flours. For example, you could combine 1 cup brown rice flour, ²/₃ cup sorghum flour, and ¹/₃ cup almond meal for a sweeter dough without the addition of sugar or honey. Or for a different flavor (but a wonderful texture) I use 1²/₃ cups garfava flour and ¹/₃ cup soy flour instead of brown rice flour. Experiment and see what taste and texture you like best.

Tapioca flour is not really a flour (it's a starch) and is pretty standard in gluten-free recipes. Quite frankly, I've not experimented with other starches for pizza crusts, but try arrowroot if you run out of tapioca flour. But if you're making gluten-free bread or cookies, potato starch flour or cornstarch works well with tapioca.

Xanthan gum is necessary in most gluten-free baking, as it replaces the stretch one gets from the gluten in regular flours.

This pizza crust recipe is so easy, I often use it to make gluten-free bread or focaccia.

Gluten-Free Bread

Place the dough in a greased loaf pan and let it rise for 30 to 40 minutes. Place the risen dough in a preheated 400-degree oven; then lower the heat to 375 degrees. Bake for 40 to 50 minutes. For a more bread-like texture, use 2 or 3 eggs instead of 4 egg whites. And experiment with different herbs or leave them out altogether.

Gluten-Free Focaccia

For this I use a spring form or casserole pan or several cake pans. Brush both the pan and the top of the dough with olive oil, make some indentations on top of the dough and sprinkle lightly with bits of tomato, olives, coarse salt, and herbs to taste. Allow dough to rise 30 minutes. Bake at 400 degrees for 30 to 40 minutes.

Dealing With Anger

Connecting Together

Natural Disasters of Anger

Discuss:

• If anger could be described as a type of natural disaster, which fits your anger style? For example, a tornado strikes suddenly and leaves suddenly. A wildfire builds in intensity and spreads. An avalanche freezes everyone out and then tumbles down. Which of these—or any other natural disaster you can think of—most resembles your anger style?

_____

_____

_____

_____

Connecting to the Topic

Roots of Anger

As you look at the following list, consider which one of these most often causes anger in your life. If the root of most of your anger is different than what's listed here, feel free to write in a new thought.

As you are comfortable, share about the root of most of your anger with your table.

- **Hurt or Pain.** When something causes us pain, we often mask the pain with anger.

- **Guilt.** If we feel guilty about something and someone calls us on it or we feel convicted internally, we may become angry.

- **Injustice.** When life is just not fair, from the plight of orphaned children to the guy who cuts us off in traffic, injustice and inequality can cause anger to rise up within us.

- **Insecurity or Rejection.** When your precious child says he hates you, when you don't get the job, insecurity and rejection can cause angry reactions that get out of control.

- **Fear.** Sometimes covering our fear with anger can make us bolder. Many times, however, fear drives us to blow up in order to get out of something scary.

_____

_____

_____

_____

_____

Connecting With God

The Bible is full of verses that can encourage us and help us stop anger in its tracks. And there are words in the Bible to address every root of anger we've considered. Take turns reading these verses aloud around the table and talking through the discussion questions that are included. If your group doesn't get through all the verses and questions, you can read through them and reflect on the questions yourself later this week.

Hurt and Pain

"He heals the brokenhearted and bandages their wounds."
(Psalm 147:3)

- When your feelings are hurt as a mom, what can you do instead of lashing out?

_____

_____

Guilt

"So now there is no condemnation for those who belong to Christ Jesus." (Romans 8:1)

- If God is not condemning you, why do we burden ourselves with feelings of guilt?

_____

_____

Injustice

"For God chose to save us through our Lord Jesus Christ, not to pour out his anger on us." (1 Thessalonians 5:9)

- How does knowing that God desires reconciliation over punishment give you a different perspective on justice?

_____

_____

Insecurity and Rejection

"I have loved you, my people, with an everlasting love. With unfailing love I have drawn you to myself." (Jeremiah 31:3)

- How does God's love and acceptance strengthen you in times of insecurity or when others reject you?

_____

_____

Fear

"And as we live in God, our love grows more perfect. So we will not be afraid on the day of judgment, but we can face him with confidence because we live like Jesus here in this world. Such love has no fear, because perfect love expels all fear. If we are afraid, it is for fear of punishment, and this shows that we have not fully experienced his perfect love." (1 John 4:17-18)

- If God's love for us is perfect, what do we have to fear? How does this help you deal with anger in times of fear?

_____

_____

Connecting to My Life

M&M® Game

1. All moms can take a little handful of M&Ms.

2. Each mom can choose one of any color to place in front of her. That's her color for this round. (Eat some of the ones you didn't choose!)

3. Go around the table and share based on how the color of candy you have for this round matches the instructions below.

4. When everyone has had a turn, choose a new color of M&M and play again. Keep playing as long as time allows.

Red = Describe a time when it was hard for you to show self-control.

Orange = Describe something that consistently makes you angry.

Brown = Describe a not-so-good choice you made when you were angry and how it made the situation worse.

Blue = Say one practical thing you do to cool off when you are angry.

Green = Say one practical way you can better show self-control before you blow your top.

Yellow = Describe a good choice you made when you were angry that helped the situation.

Additional Thoughts on Dealing With Anger

God has a lot to say about anger in the Bible. He also tells us that he is here to help us overcome our faults, including any sinful thoughts and actions when we get angry. Take some time this week to come back and read these verses and write down your answers to the question below each one.

"Understand this, my dear brothers and sisters: You must all be quick to listen, slow to speak, and slow to get angry. Human anger does not produce the righteousness God desires." (James 1:19-20)

• How do you think this verse relates to the root causes of our anger? Why does God emphasize listening here?

_____

_____

_____

"But the Holy Spirit produces this kind of fruit in our lives: love, joy, peace, patience, kindness, goodness, faithfulness, gentleness, and self-control. There is no law against these things!" (Galatians 5:22-23)

• What can you do every day to practice one of these today?

_____

_____

_____

"The temptations in your life are no different from what others experience. And God is faithful. He will not allow the temptation to be more than you can stand. When you are tempted, he will show you a way out so that you can endure." (1 Corinthians 10:13)

• How does this verse apply to your expressions of anger?

_____

_____

_____

Finally, make a praise list of all the times you could have become frustrated or lost your temper this week but didn't. Go back and encourage yourself by looking at this list whenever you need it!

_____

_____

_____

_____

_____

_____

_____

_____

_____

_____

_____

_____

A *Blessing* for *Moms*

Connecting Together

Heroes

Discuss:

- Think back to when you were a younger girl—grade school or maybe high school. Who were your heroes?

_____

_____

_____

Connecting to the Topic

A Hero Is...

What is a hero? With your group, name qualities that you think define a hero. Write those words in the space below (you'll be using them later). As you do this, think of a real human hero—not Superman or a fictional character. Only list qualities that a human being could have.

_____

_____

_____

_____

Connecting to My Life

A Superhero Blessing

You are a precious, beloved child of the one true King—the creator of the universe. Your origins are epic!

And God's love is the most powerful force in the whole world—more than all superhero powers combined!

And his love is in you and flows through you as you live out the greatest mission ever known to mankind: to love God and love others.

And on the days you don't feel like you're enough, remember that love never fails and God's love always covers you.

Believe you are a superhero with the power to influence lives for God—and be sure every woman you encounter knows this is true about her too!

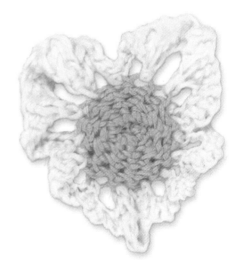

An Additional Blessing for Moms

These Bible passages were read over you during this session. Read them again this week (and as often as you like!) to remember how God truly sees you. You are loved!

"See, I have written your name on the palms of my hands." (Isaiah 49:16)

"Do not be afraid, for I have ransomed you. I have called you by name; you are mine." (Isaiah 43:1)

"My grace is all you need. My power works best in weakness." (2 Corinthians 12:9)

"For his Spirit joins with our spirit to affirm that we are God's children." (Romans 8:16)

"You made all the delicate, inner parts of my body and knit me together in my mother's womb. Thank you for making me so wonderfully complex! Your workmanship is marvelous—how well I know it. You watched me as I was being formed in utter seclusion, as I was woven together in the dark of the womb. You saw me before I was born. Every day of my life was recorded in your book. Every moment was laid out before a single day had passed. How precious are your thoughts about me, O God. They cannot be numbered! I can't even count them; they outnumber the grains of sand! And when I wake up, you are still with me!" (Psalm 139:13-18)

"And I am convinced that nothing can ever separate us from God's love. Neither death nor life, neither angels nor demons, neither our fears for today nor our worries about tomorrow— not even the powers of hell can separate us from God's love." (Romans 8:38)

"And may you have the power to understand, as all God's people should, how wide, how long, how high, and how deep his love is." (Ephesians 3:18)

Notes

A Mom's Book of Blessing